# Seeing the Need and Choosing to Lead

# Seeing the Need and Choosing to Lead

♦

## A Leadership Workbook & Guide for Real-Time Student Engagement

*Marcal A. Graham, Ed.D*

iUniverse, Inc.
New York  Lincoln  Shanghai

# Seeing the Need and Choosing to Lead
## A Leadership Workbook & Guide for Real-Time Student Engagement

Copyright © 2006, 2007 by Marcal A. Graham, Ed.D

All rights reserved. No part of this book may be used or reproduced by any means, graphic, electronic, or mechanical, including photocopying, recording, taping or by any information storage retrieval system without the written permission of the publisher except in the case of brief quotations embodied in critical articles and reviews.

iUniverse books may be ordered through booksellers or by contacting:

iUniverse
2021 Pine Lake Road, Suite 100
Lincoln, NE 68512
www.iuniverse.com
1-800-Authors (1-800-288-4677)

Because of the dynamic nature of the Internet, any Web addresses or links contained in this book may have changed since publication and may no longer be valid.

The views expressed in this work are solely those of the author and do not necessarily reflect the views of the publisher, and the publisher hereby disclaims any responsibility for them.

ISBN: 978-0-595-39989-5 (pbk)
ISBN: 978-0-595-84377-0 (ebk)

Printed in the United States of America

# *Contents*

Introduction ............................................. xi
Description of this Workbook ............................. xv

**Chapter 1**  LEADERSHIP QUESTIONNAIRE ............. 1
**Chapter 2**  REFLECTIVE ACTIVITIES .................. 9
**Chapter 3**  SCENERIOS & PROBLEM SOLVING
             SITUATIONS ............................. 14
**Chapter 4**  CRITICAL ISSUES ........................ 20
**Chapter 5**  LEADERSHIP APPLICATIONS ............... 22
**Chapter 6**  NURTURING GOOD HABITS OF
             LEADERS ................................ 24
**Chapter 7**  LEADERSHIP VIGNETTES .................. 26
**Chapter 8**  MAKING A CASE FOR LEADERSHIP ......... 29
**Chapter 9**  LEADERSHIP FOLLOW-THROUGH
             ACADEMICS & SPORTS .................... 33
**Chapter 10** GOOD DECSION MAKING & BAD
             DECISION MAKING ....................... 35
**Chapter 11** WHAT ARE YOUR POSSIBILITIES .......... 36
**Chapter 12** LEADERSHIP TIMELINE ................... 38
**Chapter 13** SOLUTIONS AND SUGGESTIONS ........... 41

Leadership Workbook Test ............................... 44
References ............................................. 47

*"I may not be able to change the world, but I guarantee I'll spark the person who does."*

*Tupac Shakur*

## PREFACE

In the fall of 2001, I had the opportunity to survey and listen to the comments of students in one of North Philadelphia's lowest achieving High Schools. This was one of many graduate research projects that consisted of collecting data for a Professor who was trying to understand the dynamics of the achievement gap from a student's perspective. Each grade ($9^{th}$-$12^{th}$) was presented with a PowerPoint presentation on how White, Latino, Asian, and African American $4^{th}$ and $8^{th}$ grade students performed on the NAEP test (Taylor-Lovelace, 2004). The data presentation clearly showed in a bar graph that African American students were the worst performing group in all academic achievement categories. In addition, each student was posed one question: What do you think is the reason why African American students performed so poorly on the test?

After thinking about this question and reviewing the dramatic display of achievement data, students' provided a laundry list of reasons as to why African American students performed poorly. The list included such responses as low expectations by teachers, peer pressure, and lack of family support. What was illuminating to me was the fact that many students in each grade level blamed themselves for not trying hard enough and lacking the motivation to want to excel in the classroom. I believe that student motivation and ownership is at the heart of the achievement gap. Moreover, I assert that by developing leadership skills within students one can alter classroom behavior and attitudes toward learning.

---

It was the day after Martin Luther King's Birthday, January $16^{th}$ 2006. I had to attend a monthly Superintendent's meeting in Southeast Washington DC to discuss the use of Professional Development and other ways to improve teaching and learning in the classroom. These meetings are always informative and engaging although they tend to last the entire day. We started the meeting with a silent prayer for Martin Luther King and recognition of his birthday the day before and his many accomplishments. Unfortunately, I had to leave a little early on this particular day. I had just missed the first bus by a mere thirty seconds and had to wait for the next Metro bus to get me back to Anacostia Station in order to catch the train.

While waiting for the bus, I witnessed four African American teenage boys joy riding in what appeared to be a stolen car. Once they circled the block a few times, I noticed that they were being chased by another car that also carried two African American male teenagers. The two cars were clearly exceeding the speed limit. Moments later, the first group of teenagers riding in the first car came around the block and crashed into the gate of a low-income housing project directly in front of me. Remember, this was a block over from the Superintendent's Meeting still taking place. The teenagers jumped out of the car and ran from the site of the crash with no visible signs of injuries. In fact, to my chagrin, they were laughing as if this was a video game they had successfully maneuvered. Approximately five minutes later, the teenagers in question returned to the site of the car crash as if nothing happened. Of course, I found myself staring in disbelief at the events that had just taken place. Each of the teenagers strolled by and made eye contact with me as if to say, "we know who you are," and I certainly knew who they were.

The question that begged to be answered as I stood waiting for the bus, and for Metro Police to show up on the scene was why weren't these kids in school? Why did they get so much enjoyment out of such mayhem? Why were they using their talents for such negative actions? I saw more than just a bunch of urban youth involved in another criminal activity; I saw the potential for leadership in these teenagers. This to me was an example of un-channeled leadership and what can happen if it is applied negatively. These teenagers were not prepared to take ownership and responsibility for their actions. It was a game in many ways rather than real life.

Furthermore, I thought, "what would happen if these teenagers used their analytical skills and determination for good rather than for destructive purposes?" I pondered what Martin Luther King would say to these kids, especially given the fact that it was a day after his birthday. I believe that holding students accountable personally and academically is the answer to many of the problems facing schools.

Leadership is an instrument that students take with them in and outside of the classroom. More importantly, it forces students to think before they act and to become better decision makers and more analytical about what happens around them. These two situations provide examples of students who have demonstrated poor leadership in the classroom and within their respective communities. I argue that this happens all too many times to students.

Moreover, I strongly believe that the answer does not exist in another Superintendent's Meeting, but rather in understanding the social realities and experiences that drive students to commit certain actions. This can only come from challenging students to be leaders and to think about every action they involve themselves in as they mature into adulthood. I have seen and heard teachers, community members, politicians and others discuss these problems across the country. What better place to start addressing issues of leadership than within students in the Nation's Capital?

---

I grew up in a community similar to the young teenagers who made the wrong choices who I just mentioned in my introduction. What made me not engage in such mayhem and self-destructive behavior? As I reflect back on my choices, I know that my mother always instilled certain values in me as child, but what about when mom was not around to guide me? What about when I was playing basketball and some guys wanted to test their manhood and demonstrate how tuff they were by starting fights and trouble? I remember that I was always expected to be a leader which meant figuring out the best solution without necessarily engaging in physical or verbal altercation.

Although I had my share of fights growing up, my mother always reminded me that I would be responsible for my actions and ultimately pay the price if I did not find an alternative to fighting. In addition, I realized that being a leader of my actions meant that I would not have many friends because I was not a follower and stayed away from crowds other than to play sports. It is because I was forced to examine group dynamics, masculinity (what it means to be tough), and the importance of grades over girls. It is those same skills that I needed in high school, as an undergraduate, in graduate school, and as I completed my doctoral studies. Moreover, young men must understand that they must make decisions at young ages that will follow them the rest of their lives. I submit that if young men view themselves as leaders, not just on the basketball court, but in every day life it will promote a different mindset and approach to learning that will re-define what it means to be strong and positive.

## WHY LEADERSHIP?

I am proposing an approach to leadership that empowers students and forces them to re-examine the amount of effort, attitude, and type of behavior they bring to the classroom on a daily basis. By engaging in this process, students can learn to take positive action, ownership, and mastery of their academic future. The ability to motivate students appears to be one of the most important factors impacting student learning and achievement. In much of my work with students I have come to realize that students not only need teachers, parents, and administrators to care about their needs, but they also need to be viewed as more than a "test score" or "statistic" but as a complete person capable of much more than making or breaking a school's adequate yearly progress. Given this reality, I then came to the conclusion that students needed to be viewed and treated as part of something more powerful and community-altering. The question that begs asking is that are we preparing our students to be leaders or good test-takers or both? Have we tapped into the passion of students? Unfortunately, the vast majority of African American students in many of our urban schools are not very good test takers according to many national and state testing assessments.

I argue that these same students are asking one definitive and reflective question as they resist traditional approaches to education which is: How can school M.O.V.E.M.E to challenge experiences, attitudes, and realities that affect me daily? Motivation, Openness, Vision, Exposure, Mastery, and Engagement are leadership qualities that will provide students with a tool for re-evaluating their economic, social, personal, and educational reality. How will students confront underlying issues that impact them personally and academically if they are not provided with a positive approach to draw from? This is outside the realm of *No Child Left Behind (NCLB) mandates,* but is needed so that students understand the value and place academic measures like NCLB and other state achievement tests say about them overtly and covertly. Moreover, they need to know that this is a very small part of actual learning which they will encounter on their educational journey. There is larger more profound thinking that they need to engage in if they are to be agents of change. If students are engaging in self-reflection academically they will have very little problem meeting the proficiency targets on many of the standardized examinations because they will aspire to the qualities needed to not only be a great student, but also a great leader.

*So to the student that says, "I want to be a surgeon" my response to them is what are you doing today to become that surgeon beyond just wanting. What kind of attitude, work ethic, vision, and leadership are you demonstrating?*

# *Introduction*

Youth leadership is not something that happens in a vacuum, but is part of a larger and more profound process. Moreover, leadership is an ongoing process that impacts decision making on a daily basis. It is our belief that leadership skills are all encompassing and academic achievement is the result of what students learn through exposure, dialogue, reflection, and hard work. Therefore, a project-based approach to leadership provides the most effective learning tool for challenging, engaging, and addressing the values and perspectives of students (Marx, 2006; Cunningham & Cordeiro 2000). Often times, students learn about leadership, if at all, too late for it to be effective. Notwithstanding proficiency on standardized examinations, students also need an understanding of group dynamics, good listening, critical thinking, problem solving skills and the ability to apply higher order thinking skills into practice which are cornerstones of good leadership.

Based on my experiences of mentoring, tutoring, teaching, conducting research and counseling of high school and college students over the past several years, I have realized that many students have underlying issues confronting their own leadership. They did not view themselves as leaders nor identified with many of the concepts associated with leadership. In addition, many of the skills and habits of mind (Costa & Kallick, 1998) that students gain through leadership are the identical skills needed to excel in higher education. Rather than concentrating solely on re-writing curriculum standards and relying on standardized tests to determine student achievement, more attention needs to be placed on performance based or authentic assessments which promote academic exploration and synthesis of information. Moreover, schools must develop strategies that address the academic, learning, and socioeconomic needs of the entire student. The answer can be found in the M.O.V.E.M.E acronym which is a holistic approach to leadership in students which can be utilized at every level of learning. Therefore, I have developed a Leadership Workbook that attempts to engage students in dialogue about the nature of leadership. This guide will challenge them to become leaders as they confront the many factors facing them in high school and throughout life.

I believe that the acronym M.OV.E.M.E. (Motivation, Openness, Vision, Exposure, Mastery and Engagement) is a critical intervention or strategy needed to inspire students to want to pursue leadership and heighten awareness. In addition, many of the qualities and habits we identify in leaders are the same qualities which can be seen in students who are successful learners. Why M.O.V.E.M.E? There are few things that inspire students into action and reflection. I believe that these are important qualities needed if we are to channel and sustain positive energy and direction.

Motivation of students continues to be an important and challenging goal for teachers, administrators, and parents alike. As we have come to recognize, students are not born to be or even envision themselves as leaders. As a result, they frown upon or are indifferent to the unwanted attention and isolation leadership may require of them. Therefore, we must promote situations, behaviors, discussions, and opportunities that demonstrate that leadership is a quality to be valued and attained.

Openness is clearly a necessary part of any dialogue with students. Environments must be created to overcome barriers and allow students to feel like they can discuss and confront any subject matter. It is through this openness that we can not only constructively critique each other, but address any underlying issues that may impede student academic, social, or emotional growth.

Vision-building is something that many students are not able to conceptualize or fail to think about the future. There is a connection between planning, preparation, and success. In order to think of yourself as a leader you must be a good planner. Vision requires having a blueprint for the future and action needed to make dreams come true. Although you may reach your goal by serendipity, most times you still need to have a plan as to where you are going as a leader.

Exposure to positive environments and roles models are critical to promoting academic excellence. Students need to understand and gain exposure to the many accomplishments of people that look like them on a daily basis. Often times, students are inundated with negative role models once they leave school and model that same behavior once they enter the classroom.

Mastery of one's actions and thoughts is a critical skill that is very important to student success. Whether in a classroom setting, part-time job, or among friends, students must recognize the importance of learning a particular task or skill to mastery. This requires knowing something beyond the surface, actually understanding the various dynamics, nuances, and levels of decision making. The question that students must ask themselves is whether they are seeking mastery over every aspect of their lives.

Engagement of youth is one of the most challenging interventions needed in order to prepare students for leadership. We must develop creative ways that that reach out to students. This may mean thinking outside of the box in order to connect with students who come from various socioeconomic backgrounds and family structures.

At the end of this Leadership Workbook, students should have a working understanding of leadership and how it impacts their daily lives. More specifically, students should recognize that leadership is not something you learn in a day, but part of something that is earned, valued, and refined over and over again. At its very least this Leadership Workbook will be a starting point for students to view themselves as leaders.

# *Description of this Workbook*

Chapter 1 consists of a leadership questionnaire (1-29) which is qualitative in nature that seeks to reveal students understanding, meanings, constructions, and perceptions of leadership. Rather than focus on specific leadership traits, we want students to think deeply and critically about how leadership impacts them directly and indirectly. By providing an open-ended question format students are able to explain in detail how leadership influences their daily interactions with family, friends, and in school.

Chapter 2 (1-20) focuses on whether students think deeply about the world around them. In addition, this chapter examines the level to which students prepare and plan for the future. They must critically examine and respond to various exercises and leadership assignments.

Chapter 3 (1-20) addresses some scenarios and problem solving issues that leaders confront on a daily basis. Sometimes students must do things that people or even friends might not agree depending on the situation.

Chapter 4 (1-7) examines many of the issues that impact students as they try to navigate through school and life. The goal of this chapter is to uncover and address many of the problems which undermine student attendance and academic progress. These issues help to demonstrate how leadership is shaped.

Chapter 5 (1-10) leadership applications requires that students actually synthesize the information about leadership and apply to particular activities that revolve around leadership.

Chapter 6 provides a model of many of the qualities needed to nurture good leaders. Many of these qualities are essential for academic excellence, the job market, and those preparing for higher education.

Chapter 7 is dedicated to presenting vignettes and skits that reinforce the importance of leadership and provide for discussion. Students assume various roles that allow them to see problems from various vantage points. In addition they are expected to analyze each play and describe the major thrust of the play and their views before and after.

Chapter 8 proposes that leadership be taught as a separate class within the Standards-Based Curriculum. Moreover, leadership is all-encompassing and should be taught as a separate discipline which placing more emphasis on the student rather than the teacher.

Chapter 9 demonstrates how Sports and Academics share many approaches to learning and preparation that students need to internalize. This Chapter provides examples on how students can take what they learn while engaging in sports in the classroom and vice versa.

Chapter 10 addresses how decision making impact the life and academic chances of students from the moment they wake up to the point at which they fall asleep. Students must examine the good and bad decisions they make and how they influence who they become, friendships they build, and ultimately their academic success.

Chapter 11 provides an opportunity for students to think about their possibilities and where they see themselves in the immediate and distant future.

Chapter 12 utilizes a Leadership Timeline which requires students to research how certain people assumed positions of leadership. In addition, this chapter also examines why students must learn the value of adversity and resiliency.

Chapter 13 examines possible solutions for the crisis affecting learning and African American males and emphasizes the role of leadership.

At the end of the book, students are given a **Leadership Test** which captures what students have gained from Leadership Workbook. It is not meant to be quantitative in nature; it does provide insight and understanding into students' beliefs, attitudes, and views of leadership.

Out of the Box Thinking & Solutions

# 1

# *Leadership Self-Questionnaire*

1. What does leadership mean to you?

2. Are you a leader at home? Explain.

Seeing the Need and Choosing to Lead

3. Do you have an older sibling who you see as a leader?

4. Have you been a leader around your friends? How?

5. What kinds of leadership positions have you had at school or in your community?

6. What are some of the qualities needed to be a good leader?

7. Are there times when you are a leader and follower? Name some instances when it happens to you.

8. Why would you <u>not</u> want to be a leader?

9. Are you afraid to be a leader? Explain

10. Has anyone ever challenged you to become a leader?

11. Do you have friends or peers who are leaders? What qualities do you admire about them?

12. Is leadership born or created? Explain.

13. Name five (5) people in Sports who you think are good leaders? How are they different?

14. Do you have a problem helping people you <u>do not</u> know?

15. Do you like speaking in front of people?




16. Are there any leadership groups or organizations within your school or community?




17. Why would you want to follow someone in a leadership position?




18. What is the best way to get people to follow you?

19. What are some of the issues leaders need to address in your community?

20. Do you work better in groups or on your own?

21. Name some times when you had to stand up for your own views?

22. When was the last time you asked for help?

23. Is it hard for you to admit when you make a mistake? Why?

## True or False

23. Leader's are able to ask for help. True or False

24. Good leaders tend to be more competitive than collaborative. True or False

25. Leadership is just for boys. True or False

26. Setting goals is something you do only in 11<sup>th</sup> grade. True or False.

**Circle the correct answer.**

27. Leadership requires the following skills which can be used in the classroom.
    1) hard work 2) courage 3) vision 4) all the above

28. Which of the following term(s) does not pertain when discussing effective leadership?
    1) vision 2) empowerment 3) selfishness

29. What communication skills do good leaders have?
    1). Listening 2). Critical Thinking 3). Public Speaking 4). All the above

Out of the Box Thinking & Solutions

# 2

## *REFLECTIVE ACTIVITIES & GOAL ATTAINMENT*

1. Do you set goals for yourself at home, school, or in your personal life?

2. What was the last goal you set for yourself?

3. What is the difference between a long-term and short-term goal? Have you set any?

4. Is setting goals a necessary part of good leadership? Why/Why not?

5. At what grade did you start preparing for college?

6. Do you set goals at the start of each school year? Each month? Each week? Each Day?

7. What is your plan for the next four years? How will you carry out that plan?

8. When was the last time you achieved your goal?

9. What kind of leader would you want to become? What must you change personally, socially, and academically about yourself in order to become that leader?

10. For a week, observe all your teachers in order to determine the leadership qualities they use when dealing with students and others. What did you find out?

11. Choose five (5) terms which best describe you and the kind of leader you aspire to be.

- Take charge
- Versatile
- Team player
- Dependable
- Empower
- Hard worker
- Like to prioritize
- Lead by example
- Need to be pushed
- Late all the time
- Lazy
- Hate working in groups
- Optimistic
- Pessimistic
- Charismatic
- Loyal
- Thinking on your feet
- Interpersonal skills
- Responsible

- Able to prioritize
- Trustworthy
- Reactive
- Proactive
- Critical of others
- Understanding
- Problem solver
- Honest
- Outspoken
- Visionary
- Tolerant
- Devoted
- Open-minded
- Procrastinator
- Critical thinker
- Impartial
- Assertive
- Aggressive

12. Take a position on an issue in your school or community and decide the best way a leader should handle it. Be ready to explain your position.

13. Leadership requires that you not only have a career plan for the future, but also have an alternative or back-up plan. What is your plan B and C when thinking about your future?

14. What are some of the things you value in life? For example, do you value hard work?

15. Name five good leaders and five bad leaders. They can be family members, in your community members, or national figures. What leadership qualities make them good or bad?

16. Do you believe that winning is always a win/lose situation? Or is it possible that everyone can win (win/win) Situation? Explain.

17. Are you motivated by intrinsic or extrinsic rewards? Which one is the most important to you? Why?

18. Are you able to be a leader even when your peers may want you to be a follower? Are you able to withstand peer pressure? What are some of your strategies for dealing with peer pressure?

19. Leaders must be able to think through problems that affect them. When was the last time you had to think through a tough personal, educational, or family-related problem?

20. When was the last time you made a decision that your friend/friends did not agree with at school?

Bonus Question: What does taking ownership of your academic ability mean to you?

Out of the Box Thinking & Solutions

# 3

# *SCENARIOS AND PROBLEM SOLVING SITUATIONS*

1. You are at a party with some of your best friends and someone passes marijuana around. You have never smoked a cigarette, much less marijuana and do not feel very comfortable now. How do you handle this situation? Can you still remain cool and keep your friends? What lessons can be learned from this situation that impact leadership?

2. You have been a B student in your first two years of high school and have been on several student organizations and after school programs. In addition, you have been working in your part-time job in the local mall over the past two years. You are in the 11$^{th}$ grade and have had some problems with Geometry and English Writing. Your grades have been dropping as a result of your various commitments. How do you handle the situation? Do you quit work or allow your grades to suffer? Which one are you going to drop? How do stop your grades from suffering? Is it possible to give your best to both?

3. Your best friend of ten years has been acting dejected and has missed some classes over the past month. He says he is doing fine, but he is visibly upset

when you confront him on his lack of school attendance. He has threatened to drop out of school or worst yet commit suicide. What do you do as a friend and as a leader?

4. Many of your friends like to cut last period class every Friday so they can go to Dave and Busters and the movies. They all want you to "hang out" but you must pass this class with a B or better in order to be on the honor roll. What do you do?

5. You have a test on Friday and somehow one of your classmates has a copy of the test. What do you do?

6. Have you ever been asked to do something that goes against your value system?

7. You feel like a teacher has just talked to you in a disrespectful manner? How do you handle the situation?

8. You have been appointed the new leader of the Hip Hop Group of your community. It is a well-known group that performs at different events in your school and around the community. Although the group is good, they

16   Seeing the Need and Choosing to Lead

have the ability to be much better. Moreover, the group has a negative attitude and is not motivated when it comes to learning new steps in order to get better. In addition, there seems to be no imagination when it comes to thinking about the direction of the group. Another problem is that the two previous leaders were afraid to admit that they made mistakes to the group. As a leader of this group, what do you do to change this situation? Remember you must address all the facts of the case.

9. A couple of your best friends have asked you to steal a pair of Air Jordan sneakers. Since many of the 'fly" and 'cool' students have these same pair of sneakers, do you feel pressured to steal a pair? What are the consequences of your behavior? How do you handle the situation?

10. A teacher just made the following comment to you: "You have been a "C" student for most of the school year and I do not expect much more from you." Do you try to prove her wrong and work harder or do you live up to her expectations?

11. You want to impress a girl in your Math Class, so you think the best way to do this is by making fun of other students and not studying. Is this the correct approach? What are the short-term and long-term issues you must consider?

12. You are on the bus with your friends and someone from another school pushes you intentionally because they are jealous of your new outfit or sneakers. What do you do? In another situation, a close friend of yours feels that by insulting you they can impress a girl/boy in your class. How do you diffuse the situation?

13. A fight just "broke out" in the cafeteria and your best friend is involved in the fight. What should you do first: 1) help your friend, 2) run the other way, 3) go and get help, 4) stand by and watch? Explain your answer.

13. Please explain the following statement,"Poor choices equal poor life chances."

14. A very close friend of yours has just brandished a knife and wants you to hold it in your locker until after school. What do you say to your friend? Do you notify your teachers? What are the pros and cons of your actions?

15. If you played basketball which position would you play and why? What kinds of leadership skills would you need at your position? What kinds of leadership skills would you need if you played tennis? Compare and Contrast the two sports and the kind of leadership skills that are needed.

16. Take some time and think about some of your bad study habits. Develop a plan on how to change those habits for one month. After two weeks report on any positive differences you have made in how you approach studying in two of your major classes. Keep a daily log on your study habits.

17. Define what self-discipline means to you. How many times do you practice self-discipline in your everyday life and in school? Is it a necessary part of success?

18. It appears that many teenagers are not able to control or manage their anger when placed in hostile or confrontational situations. Can you name a situation/s where you were able to control your anger? How were you able to do this? Name some ways you can channel your anger in a positive fashion. Create an anger management skit with some of your classmates where you all portray angry students and demonstrate positive avenues for handling a particular situation.

19. Have you ever thought more than twice about a decision you made? Leaders should always think before they act or make a decision. Every decision you make has a consequence no matter how big or small. Spend one day thinking about many of the decisions you have made and how things turned out as result.

20. What does it mean to you when you step into the classroom? Do you look to score or pass?

Out of the Box Thinking & Solutions

# 4

# *CRITICAL ISSUES IMPACTING STUDENT LEARNING*

1. Do you feel safe in your school?

2. What would you do if your friend stole a car? Would you ride with him/her? Would you tell the Police? Would you keep it a secret?

3. Do you know anyone who has been harassed?

4. Do you know anyone who has committed suicide or homicide?

5. When was the last time you stood up for what you believe in? Provide some times when you have had to stand-up?

6. How do you communicate with people?

7. Name some ways you have empowered others?

Out of the Box Thinking & Solutions

# 5

# *LEADERSHIP APPLICATIONS & PROJECTS*

1. Take what you have learned about the value of Leadership and create your own leadership manual for your classmates and peers to follow. What is the foundation of your book? What are the most important skills or values a person should walk way understanding once they read your manual? What are some do's and don'ts?

2. Develop a leadership game that involves creativity teamwork, and critical thinking. This could be a game along the lines of Jeopardy, Wheel of fortune or a card game.

3. How would you inspire others in your community to seek positions of leadership in your community?

4. Start a Spelling Bee with your classmates that incorporates many of the words found in leadership.

5,  Create a poster presentation that captures the leadership responsibilities you have been part of over the past few years.

6.  Develop a leadership crossword puzzle that utilizes key leadership concepts such as: collaboration, consensus, and extrinsic rewards to name a few.

7.  Create your own leadership cartoon strip that addresses issues of leadership impacting society. It can be funny or serious, but must be analytical and reflective in nature.

8.  Develop a leadership needs assessment for your class, school, or community.

9.  If you were building a website for student leaders what would it look like? How would you reach other student leaders? What links would you have? Conferences?

Out of the Box Thinking & Solutions

# 6

# *NURTURING GOOD HABITS OF LEADERS*

A successful model of leadership must center on certain habits in order to be successful. While there are several leadership models one can follow, I think that Stephen Covey's (1989) discussion of the 7 habits of highly effective people provides some great direction for students who strive for leadership. With the help of Covey's work (1989), I have developed (6) new categories that students can follow in the classroom and as they pursue leadership:

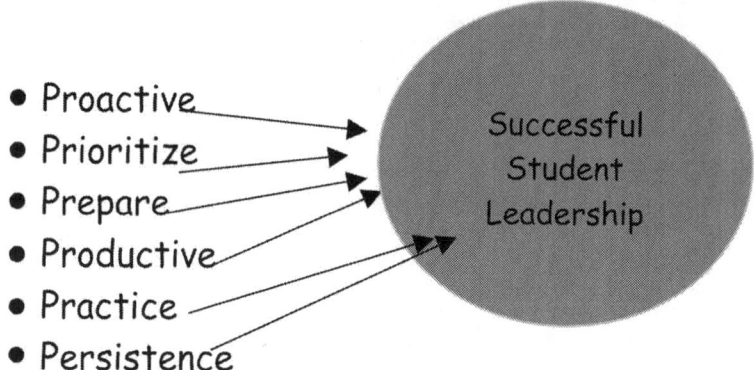

- Proactive
- Prioritize
- Prepare
- Productive
- Practice
- Persistence

→ Successful Student Leadership

If students are proactive in their approach to learning they greatly enhance their chances of achieving their goals. This requires prioritizing goals so that things are accomplished in a timely fashion. In addition, students must understand that preparation (i.e. short-term and long-term planning) is critical as they embark on the unknown. In order to be productive in all academic pursuits, students must strive for excellence and channel energy and resources in order to reach new levels of academic and personal achievement. By the time students reach college, many of them lack the habits, skills, and mindset needed to negotiate the academic, economic, and personal demands in higher education. What is also apparent is that students must view persistence and hard work as important building blocks of leadership and learning. This cycle that students can follow has application in all subjects. If teachers utilize logs or spend time reflecting with students on whether they have been proactive, prioritized, have prepared, practiced, and been persistent for class, then students will internalize these qualities.

Out of the Box Thinking & Solutions

# 7

# *Leadership Vignettes*

*Leadership Skits* or *Vignettes* are opportunities that allow students to act and assume roles that involve them assuming positions of leadership. Moreover, students need to deconstruct and understand the rationale behind why they must strive for leadership in their personal and academic life. In addition, they must understand that it follows them in everyday life and is not something they turn on and off again like a light switch.

## What is leadership?

| | |
|---|---|
| Terry: | Why do we need to be a leader? |
| James: | I think being a leader if stupid? |
| Eric: | Why! |
| Tina: | I think it is much easier to follow people (excitedly). |
| Kim: | I agree. You do not have to think much because other people do it for you. |
| Terry: | I feel like being a leader can be a good thing (wondering aloud) |
| James: | Why do you think so? |
| Terry: | People want to follow you! |
| Eric: | Why would people follow you? |
| Tina: | I have a lot to say and I am funny too. |
| James: | People will follow you because you are funny? What if you are smart? |
| Terry: | Yes, people like to follow you if you are smart. |
| Tina: | Do you think I can be a leader? |

Kim: Yes, because you are smart, funny, and nice to people.
James: To be a leader I need to be nice to people?
Terry: Sure.

**Leadership Analysis**: What did we learn from this leadership skit? What did you learn about leadership?

## Can Leaders be Cool Too

Timothy: I think some kids who are leaders are boring.
Tiffany: How come?
Timothy: They study too much and think they know everything.
Sandra: Ditto (emphatically).
Gregg: Why do you feel this way Timothy?
Timothy: I was trying to listen to these kids debate on the value of school uniforms I could not understand many of the points they were trying to make.
Kim: And, what does that mean. (laughing)
Reginald: Just because you know a lot of information about an issue and believe in it does not make you boring.
Timothy: I never thought about like that.
Gregg: I think it is cool to know a lot of information about a subject and express your opinions about it.
Sandra: In order to know a lot about an issue you must do your homework so you can be smart and cool when you talk to your friends.
Timothy: I guess I should have listened to them talk more. Huh!
Tiffany: I think so.
Reginald: There is always a next time.

**Leadership Analysis**: Before you read this vignette, did you feel like you could be a leader and be cool? Can you be both? Why or why not?

## The Leadership Trap

| | |
|---|---|
| Kim: | I like Will because he is always having fun. |
| Diamond: | Yeah, but Will does not like to go to class and when he does he is always playing around when the teacher is talking. |
| Kerry: | He is really funny and is really popular in school. |
| Thomas: | Will is a really good basketball player and wears 'fly' clothes. |
| Kim: | I think it would be cool to hang out with a guy like Will. |
| Diamond: | It appears that you want to hang out with him for all the wrong reasons. |
| Dave: | What's wrong with being around someone who is popular? |
| Thomas: | Isn't being popular and a leader the same thing? |
| Daisy: | I have been listening to everyone and I believe that just because you are popular does mean you are the kind of person who should lead. |
| Diamond: | We need to always think and ask ourselves why people are following a person or what kind of personal qualities does that individual have. |
| Daisy: | If we don't ask questions we might end up the same way. |
| Kim: | Yeah, I just found out that Will is failing most of his classes. |
| Thomas: | I see what you mean. |
| Dave: | I guess if anything Will should follow us. |
| Daisy: | Now that is a thought. |

**Leadership Analysis**: What did you learn from this leadership skit? What did you learn about leadership? Do you know anyone like Will? Have you ever followed someone because they were popular?

Out of the Box Thinking & Solutions
# 8

# *Making a Case for Leadership Infusion*

Leadership Skills as a part of the curriculum: What can be gained?

> *"In public education we don't ask kids to think"*
> *District of Columbia Educational Administrator, 2006*

I strongly argue that Leadership Skills are more transformational and all-encompassing and provide for a fuller and richer educational experience which not only prepares students to be life-long learners, especially with the use of performance based or authentic assessments. It allows you to challenge students about their perceptions and core values and actually see immediate results. Rather than focus on making sure a student understands a particular concept, the student in question takes ownership of making sure they understand what is taught. Once we identify the values that students have, we can start to slowly disarm negative attitudes, and build up the kinds of leadership and character-building qualities that facilitate the following character traits:

- Critical thinking
- Peer Editing
- Study Skills
- Academic Achievement
- Listening
- Planning

- Thinking on Your Feet
- Writing
- Public Speaking
- Character Issues & Values/How do you respond in challenging situations
- Adversity
- Sports/Real Life
- Conflict Resolution
- Testing Preparation
- A Heavy Dose of Reading
- Interpersonal Skills
- Trust Building

In the book, Transformative Curriculum Leadership, Henderson and Hawthorne (2006) provide an engaging and informative approach in their discussion of curriculum that is thinking centered and performance based:

Mainstream Curriculum Philosophy

- Pre-determined skill based and content-based subject learning
- Use of standardized instructional outcomes
- Reliance on standardized tests
- Learning obedience to authority
- Learning cooperative/complaint behaviors in the context of a competitive educational meritocracy

Transformative Curriculum Philosophy

- Thinking-centered subject learning using constructivist activities
- Use of multi-literate expressive outcomes

- Reliance on personally tailored performance-based tests
- Learning diversified, lifelong inquiry responsibilities
- Learning informed, democratic citizenship related to equity, civility, and diversity.

(Henderson & Hawthore, page 5)

In examining the Transformative Curriculum presented by Henderson and Hawthorne (2006), it provides a blueprint for empowerment and the type goals I would like to incorporate into leadership training for students. Currently, many traditional public schools are more concerned about student performance on standardized test rather than making sure that students have learned how to consistently engage in higher-order thinking. What is even more important is providing the kind of curriculum that allows students to see themselves as something greater than a test score, but also expected to excel in academic and personal endeavors.

As I examine the achievement gap, I assert that educators are approaching student achievement from the wrong vantage point. Although there are factors such as family background, teacher quality, and school culture which are barriers that affect the achievement gap, one important group is not addressed when critics point to the many educational problems impacting urban students. The group in question are students and their desire to want to succeed in the face of adversity and other obstacles.

What we are left with is one question, how do we harness and motivate students to want to learn beyond the threshold of "just giving enough" to get by academically? Clearly, in order to be competitive students will need to master important academic, higher-order, and analytical skills which not only allow for excellence on standardized test, but that also promotes self-reflection and imagination. On a more basic level, if one student is spending their spare time learning algebraic equations and another student is watching television, it not hard to imagine which one will come out knowing more about how to master algebra.

In order to close any achievement gap, students will need to spend more of their time trying to master skills that they either are very weak in or lack altogether. Consequently, closing the achievement gap is not simply about the teaching and learning that take place in the classroom, but is more importantly also about student's efforts and determination that must happen outside of the classroom. More succinctly, the ability to inspire students to want to read even when it not required or to work on math problems in their spare time is the missing ingredient that will lead to closing the achievement gap.

Out of the Box Thinking & Solutions

# 9

## *Leadership Follow-Through: Academics & Sports: What do they have in common? A Commitment to Mastery*

Sports and academics share many commonalities one being the need to have students committed to each endeavor. If we examine for example we see that in order to become a better free throw shooter in the sport of basketball which is a team sport, one must practice, be mechanically sound, and follow-through with the shot. They must continue this form whether they are wide open or have a defender in front of them. More specifically, thy must be able to perform under pressure in many situations. One aspect of basketball that is even more interesting is the free throw that players must make while screaming fans are waving items to obstruct one's vision as they prepare to shoot the ball.

In the sport of tennis, players are out there in front of fans as they hit the ball hoping that the other person makes a mistake while attempting to hit the ball over the net. In a close match every point is critical and a player must be able to deal with the intensity that comes with each passing point. Unlike basketball, tennis players must showcase or perform in front of a stadium of people and motivate themselves emotionally and psychically throughout the course of the match. Each player must understand and take advantage of the weaknesses of the other player. Having heart, desire, being highly motivated, the internal motivation to win is ever present.

What do these two sports have to do with the achievement gap? I would say that they have everything to do with it. Many students, especially many African American students lack the intrinsic motivation, mechanics, and the follow-through to be high achieving learners. I argue that if we approach teaching and learning more like sports such as basketball and tennis we might have a different type of student. In order to master certain skills, students must put in the time and strive for excellence. Therefore, schools must provide activities that model behavior, reward systems, and drill test taking skills, homework, and more importantly a positive attitude toward learning. In addition, there must be incentives that promote student achievement in all subject areas. Students need to see themselves more as professional athletes who must improve their game or learning even when they are not on the floor or performing in front of people. Consequently, practice or preparation (i.e. homework, tutors, mentors, reading the newspaper, attending the library, doing practice tests provides the time necessary for students to master certain skills. In addition, students must not only learn to identify their own weaknesses, but also work on behaviors that promote academic self-reflection and introspection. This would operate as the practice level.

The next level would be considered the mechanical level where students would work on refining their study habits, problem solving, critical thinking, and approaches to learning. Are they maximizing their true capacity for learning? Do they study at all? Do they study hard or study smart? Often times students open a book, but are not fully engaged in identifying the main idea in a reading passage, realizing what the author is talking about, or where supporting information exist. Are students taking the time to learn vocabulary words and how they should be utilized in the text? In terms of mathematics, students will need to spend time mastering the basics such as: 1). fractions, 2) percents, 3) and algebraic equations.

At the next stage students need to be able put the time into becoming a master student through continuous practice and must also be mechanically sound. In addition, students must be able to follow-through with every obstacle, project, and personal or professional endeavor they confront. Moreover, students must be able to take the knowledge they have acquired, developed strong and steady work, and study habits (i.e. critical thinking and higher order thinking skills that lead to mastery of material. Follow-through is critical because it forces students to put what they have learned to the test. This will usually be done under pressure in testing situations. Furthermore, students need to learn to make good decisions when placed in academic, professional, and personal challenging situations.

What I am proposing is that the teachers operate more like content coaches and motivators and put much of the responsibility on students to perform rather than teachers doing the work for them. Teachers must develop and provide incentives that drive students to want to aspire to academic success.

Out of the Box Thinking & Solutions

# 10

# *Leadership: Good Decision Making vs. Bad Decision Making*

It appears that many students find themselves making mistakes that they can often side-step if they practice good decision making in their personal and academic life. While curiosity is a part of growth, students must still reflect on whether being curious will cause irrevocable harm to harm to them in the short-term and long-term. I assert that students spend too much time trying to recover from many of the decisions they make on a daily basis. No matter how big or small these decisions have repercussions that can impact an individual for the rest of their lives.

Therefore, I am proposing that students devote time to understanding the implications of the decisions they make throughout the course of the day, week, and month. In doing this, students should look for patterns in their own behavior and spend time reflecting on situations when they demonstrated poor judgment or bad decision making academically and with friends. Have there been times when you believed that you made good decisions? What is preventing you from making good decisions most of the time? What are some steps that you need to take to ensure that you make the best decisions in your academic and personal life?

Out of the Box Thinking & Solutions
# 11

## *What Are Your Possibilities?*

Many times students do not spend quality time thinking about what they are capable of accomplishing academically, professionally, or personally. More specifically, students do not know what they can accomplish because many do not dedicate time, resources, and energy to mastering skills that are necessary to reach excellence. Name some instance when you have thought about what your possibilities were? What things could you achieve?

Often times, urban youth are committed to immediate ways of climbing out of poverty. With limited opportunities and life chances many believe that there are short ways of reaching economic success. The "hoop dream" or "blowing up overnight" as a rap star or basketball and football star has continued to grow in mass appeal to many African American males. It is a double-edged sword that does not seem to be losing its unspoken message as teachers, parents, community residents, and concerned citizens confront this reality. On one hand you, want children and teenagers to dream beyond their immediate surrounding and see themselves achieving greatness whether in sports or in life. Conversely, when does dreaming undermine actual day-to-day learning and impede a student's ability to confront the demands of academic excellence.

As educators, I do not think we have done a good job deconstructing the economic of what African American students dream about and channel financial, but more importantly invaluable time, and brain power into trying to capture. More specifically, we have not forced our students to plan for the future personally or professionally. We have not made them ask the question? Why should I read more? What kind of reward will I get? Why is it important? We have not had the "Ah Hah" moments where students say look basketball is nice and I enjoy it tremendously, but understanding calculus will make me money over my lifetime with less physical exertion. Or the ability to be an analytical thinker and reader will allow me to become president of my own company. Moreover, we have not forced students to confront the underlying reasons behind why they are where they are economically and the repercussions of tomorrow. We must challenge students to want more out of life, but at the same time they need to be able to dream the impossible. They need to know that they can create positive avenues for creating wealth in their communities. They have pride and need positive reinforcement.

As I matured, I observed Mr. Sam, a successful African American man, who ran the corner store in my old neighborhood in North Philadelphia. I saw him adding numbers in this head as he dealt with the many distributors who would bring items to his store. I also watched older African American men who were owners of the barbershop in the neighborhood. In addition, I saw these same men in the classroom as teachers and as principals. I was always a dreamer, but always believed that education would get me to wherever I wanted to be in life. I have not looked back since.

Many people posed the question about whether athletes were role models or not? I believe a better question that should be posed to African American students is what road should I choose to follow? It is apparent that the youth love to watch and mimic sports and entertainment icons, but they must understand all aspects of the person and make a choice as to whether they want to follow certain types of behaviors. They must understand that there are positive and negative consequences.

Out of the Box Thinking & Solutions

# 12

## *Leadership Timeline*

Please provide the times and accomplishments of the following great leaders. Why were they great leaders during their times? What can we learn today? Who would you like to be more like as you pursue leadership?

- Ralph Bunche
- Franklin Delano Roosevelt
- William E.B. Dubois
- Ronald Regan
- Margaret Thatcher
- Mary McLeod Bethune
- Hillary Clinton
- Booker T. Washington
- Benjamin Banneker
- Charles Richard Drew
- Dwight Eisenhower
- George Bush
- Arthur Ashe
- Madeline Albright

- Arthur Schomburg
- Paul Robeson
- Toussaint L'Ouverture
- Henry Ossawa Tanner
- John Hope Franklin
- General Alexandre Dumas
- Zora Neale Thurston
- Horace Mann

## Adversity & Resiliency

The ability to turn a negative situation into a positive is the hallmark of great leader. Everyday we are confronted with situations that force us to re-think our actions at that specific time. The true test of a person's character is not when life is rosy, but how they respond when they are confronted with a family loss, performed poorly on an examination, did not get accepted in to the school of their choice, or you did not play your best game. All these instances demonstrate how adversity can be the impetus for igniting greatness or the thread that unravels when we pull on it.

In the field of sports we can see clear examples of individuals either embracing adversity, but very rarely are we provided with a door or lens to see how people confront leadership on a daily basis. I am always amazed at the students I have come in contact with on overtime and the adverse situations they had to overcome to just arrive at the door steps of higher education, high, middle, and elementary school.

How do we take a negative experience or interaction in one-on-one or group situation and develop a plan for dealing with it? Have you ever thought about how you react to adverse situations? Do you consider yourself resilient? When was the last time you had to recover from your academic, personal, or professional failures? How did your attitude about a particular situation impact your ability to be successful?

Out of the Box Thinking & Solutions

# 13

# *Reflective Thoughts & Solutions*

The need to fill in the gaps that schools are not capable of addressing such as motivation, reward, and personal growth are critical to academic excellence. The inability of students to make connections about there socio-political and economic realities in the classroom and the issues of class, and race to a lesser degree continues to have the most detrimental impact on student learning. Students do not have the institutional memory or experiences to understand the things taking place around them. The current curriculum is not set-up in away to connect with the minds and hearts of students given their home life and experiences (Tatum, 2005). It can not motivate them to be positive agents of change because they lack ability to articulate the economic, political, and social realties of their environment. Moreover, there is a learning mismatch taking place where students are not able to fully apply what is learned in the classroom to what is learned at home and vice versa.

What lens are students using to make sense of their world? I posit that students at the k-12 level in under performing public schools already have the capacity to excel at math and science and have a hunger for knowledge, but are not motivated to channel that hunger properly. The answer will only come from honest conversations that revolve around leadership and personal accountability.

If we look at the crisis impacting African American boys it too is connected to a need for effective and ongoing leadership. More specifically, what is needed is a venue for boys to view themselves as leaders and to build community, and to destroy negative perceptions of themselves. Offer leadership training to African American boys, so that they see themselves as leaders so that they make better decisions as they progress through life. Students need better reward systems in order to motivate them into action.

Unfortunately, many public schools seem to be moving at a snails pace while other sectors of our society are responding daily to the changing demands of the global economy. The illusive goal of student achievement will only come if we find new ways to connect with students. Consequently, this will require confronting many of the beliefs and values that African American children embrace. The inability of African American children to discriminate between fact and fiction (reality versus make believe) continues to be an ongoing problem in the classroom. In some ways these images on television, radio, and video fill a void that is missing in many African American families. We must develop ways to motivate student to learn. Parents are raising children, but other forms of interaction are just as important in rearing children.

Students need positive social activities, club, and outlets to have fun that promote and drive academic success. Where are the carrots in public education for students to want to succeed? If they come intrinsically motivated we have very little to worry about, but many do not. What carrots do you have for them? The stick is not working because students know how much they can get away with and what the system will allow such as suspensions and expulsions. Can the good students get rewarded? What about a ceremony for students who made the honor roll and Spelling Bee competition. Exposure is the key element in how students make decisions.

In summary, I believe that students never really reach their academic potential because they very rarely strive for the level of seriousness and motivation needed to overcome learning weaknesses. In order to overcome obstacle in a student's personal and professional life they will have to pursue not only excellence, but understand that adversity and resiliency are necessary characteristics of their survival. If look at the state of public education, they have only recently made the connection that students must not only perform higher-order thinking in the classroom and in everyday life.

More importantly, I argue that developing student leadership while it is not a cure all, it does indeed provide an intervention for re-engaging students learning and is also an instrument for reaching the hearts, minds, and souls of students. Teaching effective leadership is transformational and forces students to challenge how they see the world around rather than accepting the status quo. In addition, one of the goals of student leadership is allowing them to recognize that they indeed have a critical role in their success and failure. The fact is that no one will care that they came from a single-parent home, was poor, a minority, or was poorly educated, but they will care is you find positive ways for overcoming obstacles in your path. I believe the slogan "No Excuses" is very appropriate in that it allows students to understand that no one is going to feel sorry for them if they fail to reach their intended goals, especially if they did not give one-hundred percent to their educational undertaking.

Out of the Box Thinking & Solutions

# *Leadership Workbook Test*

**Part One**

1. What did you gain from this book?

2. What were some of the leadership themes that you learned from this book?

3. How will you apply these leadership concepts to your family, school, or life?

4. Do you feel like you are ready to be a leader? Explain.

5. Are you a transformational or transactional leader?

6. Has studying leadership made you think about leadership differently?

# LEADERSHIP WORKBOOK
## Part Two

**Please Check the Box.**

| | | | | |
|---|---|---|---|---|
| Do you think that leadership is something you should strive for? | Strongly Disagree | Somewhat Disagree | Somewhat Agree | Strongly Agree |
| Are you ready to do what is necessary to become a good leader? | Strongly Disagree | Somewhat Disagree | Somewhat Agree | Strongly Agree |
| Do you feel like you learned a lot about leadership? | Strongly Disagree | Somewhat Disagree | Somewhat Agree | Strongly Agree |
| Will peer pressure stop you from becoming a leader? | Strongly Disagree | Somewhat Disagree | Somewhat Agree | Strongly Agree |
| Did you find it easy to apply what you learned from studying leadership in your real life? | Strongly Disagree | Somewhat Disagree | Somewhat Agree | Strongly Agree |

# *References*

Cunningham, W. & Cordeiro, P. (2000). Educational Administration: A Problem-Based Approach. Allyn and Bacon: Boston.

Costa, A., & Kallick, B. (2000). Habits of Mind: A Developmental Series, Association for Supervision and Curriculum Development: Virginia.

Covey, Stephen. (1989). *The 7 Habits of Highly Effective People*. Free Press: New York.

Ellis, Dave. (2003). *Becoming a Master Student*. Houghton Mifflin Company: Boston.

Henderson, James & Hawthorne, Richard. (2006). Transformative Curriculum Leadership. New Jersey: Prentice Hall.

Marx, Gary (2006). *Future-Focused Leadership:* Preparing Schools, Students, And Communities for Tomorrow's Realities, Association for Supervision and Curriculum Development: Virginia.

Maxwell, John. (1993). *Developing the Leader Within You*. Thomas Nelson Publishers: Nashville.

Tatam, Alfred. (2005). Teaching Reading to Black Adolescent Males: Closing the Achievement Gap, Stenhouse Publishers: Maine.

Taylor-Lovelace, Kay. (2004). *Through Their Eyes: A Strategic Response to the National Achievement Gap*, Research for Better Schools, Philadelphia.

978-0-595-39989-5
0-595-39989-4

Made in the USA
Lexington, KY
02 April 2013